CAPTAIN RICKENBACKER'S STORY

*Of the Ordeal and Rescue of Himself
and the Men With Him*

AS TOLD TO THE PRESS
ON DECEMBER 19, 1942

Privately Printed by

THE AMERICAN BRAKE SHOE
AND FOUNDRY COMPANY

230 Park Avenue, New York

1943

Eddie Rickenbacker

NOTE

Few stories of the War can compare for drama, courage, and epic quality with that of Captain Eddie Rickenbacker and the men who spent 21 days with him on emergency life rafts in the South Pacific.

Many of us will want to read this story, as Captain Rickenbacker himself tells it, and to draw from it the inspiration of the will to win that these men demonstrated. We will want to keep it, and to show it to our children, as an example of American courage, American faith, and American ideals in 1942.

WM. B. GIVEN, JR.
President

WASHINGTON, DEC. 19.—*Following is the complete text of the remarks of Captain Eddie Rickenbacker at the press conference of Henry L. Stimson, Secretary of War, today:*

FIRST let me say that I am grateful for the personal interest that you have shown in our case and the many courtesies you have shown to my wife and family, the confidence that you have helped to instill in them in the eventual outcome. To the press I am grateful for the many expressions, friendly expressions, that I understand have gone forth.

All of us are happy to say that we are indebted deeply to our own Air Forces, to the Marines, and to the boys of our Navy for our presence here today. Particularly the Navy, which had the greater share of the burden. They gave us their energy unstintingly day and night when we needed it so badly. The one unfortunate note is that we couldn't bring all the men back.

One young man, Sergeant Alexander T. Kaczmarczyk, a Polish boy, was lost. I was fortunate to be able to bring back Colonel Hans Adamson. I brought him back on a hospital bed. We brought back Sergeant James W. Reynolds, radio operator, whom we left in San Francisco in a hospital well along the way toward recovery. That is his home and his parents were there to meet him. I think he will be all right in a week or two.

Colonel Adamson is still quite a sick man because of the many things he went through. Not only did he have a very bad time, but on arrival in the Samoans from another member of a group of islands, he showed up a very bad case of diabetes. At the time the hospital did not have any insulin, but there happened to be a doctor who came in that particular day who was a diabetic, with a personal supply, and he saved the situation. Colonel Adamson then unfortunately developed pneumonia; we almost lost him again. Then I started west. During my absence of ten days he developed lung trouble—an abscess on the lung— and he had to be operated on. But on my return he seemed to show improvement. It was unbelievable. By staying over a couple of days more,

I was able, happily so, to load him on board the ship and bring him through. He is now in Walter Reed Hospital and in good hands. I am certain that, being back in Washington among his friends and family, within six weeks or two months he will have recuperated and become normal again.

Tells Story from Beginning

There are a lot of things I can't tell you, as you gentlemen understand. They are of vital military importance, but I will try and give you as much of the story as I can in detail. The simplest way I know of doing that is to tell you what happened from the start.

We arrived in Hawaii by clipper. We left that evening. We were going to leave for our first destination, which was in the south Pacific, at 10:30 a.m. As we were taking off the hydraulic system let go on the left-hand brake, and it looked as if we were going to take down all the hangars at Hickam Field. We had to ground-loop into the runway. I was informed there was another

[9]

ship available and that by switching the equipment, baggage and mail, we would be ready to go, and were, about 1:30 a.m. It was a beautiful night. I went to bed in the rail end of the B-17 on a cot.

I awakened in the morning about 6:30 and went into the cockpit. Everything was serene. The ship was purring along beautifully, and we were due to land at this island at 9:40. At 10:30 we hadn't seen it. In the meantime I was a little bit worried; the navigator was worried, and so was the pilot. I asked them if they had called for bearings, and that was when we found we had difficulty with our radio system. Not only that—after double checking our compass we found the compass had not been swung and that the outfit was off several degrees, which complicated our problem.

Plane Overshot its Mark

I felt and said at the time that I thought we had overshot, because I felt we had more of a tail wind than the boys thought they had. Mind you,

Captain Rickenbacker and the men with him left Hawaii in a Flying Fortress similar to the ship shown above.

Captain Eddie Rickenbacker being lifted from the rescue plane. This was one of the first pictures of the rescue to reach the United States.

there were no weather stations like those in this country, no teletype to get the weather around; it is all based on long-range forecast and isn't always as accurate as it might be. I definitely feel that condition will be eliminated and improved upon in the very near future.

We kept flying and finally decided to try the old box method of locating something, looking for a ship, an island. Under those conditions you get what out there they call island-eyes—you see land from many different angles and it is nothing more than cloud shadows. But when you want to find land and are anxious to see it you multiply it tenfold. We had that problem, but time was fleeting and our gas supply was running low. We didn't know where we were and we knew that no one else knew. There wasn't anything we could do about it but keep going, hoping we would run into something. It finally got down to where we shut off two outside engines to save our gas and cruised along on the two inside ones and our last message out was that we had an hour's gas left, approximately.

Dropped Mail, Tools, Baggage

We then started to pound out the SOS. Our radio operator did that for one solid hour. In the meantime we dropped everything in the way of mail, tools, baggage and equipment that was loose in the ship, and if you ever think that material things are worth anything, ladies and gentlemen, have that experience and you will find out how useless they are no matter how you may have cherished them.

We put our water and rations in the radio compartment; the mattresses we put up against the wall to cushion the shock, and through expert piloting on the part of Captain William T. Cherry, plus a lot of good luck, we went into a trough and landed up against the big swell. We might have been so unfortunate as to have hit the top of the swell and we would have gone on down.

Colonel Hans C. Adamson got a sprained back out of it; the radio operator got a badly bumped nose. There were five of us in the radio compartment, and when he hit we didn't skid very far, as you can appreciate. It was rather sudden and none too comfortable a shock, and a portion of our radio, which was on the wall in the tail end, let go and came up and broke down the door into the compartment, and that upset things, with Colonel Adamson's sprained back and the fact that when the boat on my side was kicked out the raft got tangled in the ropes.

No Water and Only Four Oranges

I can say frankly that all of us were so anxious to get away from the ship before she sank we didn't pay much attention to our rations. We had no water when we went off and we had no food. We saved four oranges, and they were scrawny ones at that, which we lived on for eight days. I carved up those oranges into eight pieces and rationed them out, and if you ever had seven hungry pairs of eyes watching you carve, you prove to be a pretty good carver, even though you haven't got the facilities—the parts were pretty well balanced.

Unfortunately, the little boat, the two-man boat upset, and this boy we lost went overboard. He swallowed some salt water and was violently seasick for several hours, which didn't contribute to reducing his thirst any; it multiplied it. Several of us were feeling none too good because it was rough. The boy got to drinking salt water during the night, unbeknown to us, and between salt water poisoning and starvation, we lost him on the night of the 13th.

I had taken a piece of rope out of the ship and we tied the boats together about twenty feet apart. We put Captain Cherry and the co-pilot, Second Lieutenant James C. Whittaker, and the radio operator in the front one; Colonel Adamson and the little engineer, Private John F. Bartek, and myself in the middle, and the navigator and crew chief, Sergeant Kaczmarczyk in the other.

After we got going naturally we got to thinking about our food and water, but we didn't dare go back to the ship for fear she would sink and suck us down with it. Then we ran into a five-day calm, which left the ocean like a mirror. It was beastly hot. Most of the boys had thrown off their shoes and some their socks, and that was unfortunate. They felt they might have to swim, but it turned out they had their feet and legs burned very badly. Two or three of them had nothing but a jumper on, no hats. I was more fortunate. I had a pair of high-top shoes on account of my bum foot and an old felt hat that Mrs. Rickenbacker had been trying to get me to get rid of for the last ten years. It proved to be very valuable. I filled it with salt water and pulled it down before my eyes. I had grabbed three or four handkerchiefs and we passed these around and put them around our nose and face, bandit fashion, which helped, but it was very hard on our hands and face, and feet, particularly.

No Rain Until Eighth Night

We had no rain until the eighth night. We saw nothing in the way of searching planes nor ships. The little boy in my boat had an issue Bible in the pocket of his jumper, and the second day out we organized little prayer meetings in the evening and morning and took turn about reading passages from the Bible, and frankly and humbly we prayed for our deliverance. After the oranges were gone there showed up a terrific lot of pangs of hunger, and we prayed for food.

We had a couple of little fish lines with hooks about the size of the end of my little finger but no bait, and if it wasn't for the fact that I had seven witnesses, I wouldn't dare tell this story because it seems so fantastic. Within an hour after prayer meeting a sea gull came in and landed on my head, and you can imagine my nervousness in trying to turn around and get him, which I did. We wrung his head and feathered him and carved up his carcass, distributed it, and used his innards for bait.

Captain Cherry caught a little mackerel about six or eight inches long and I caught a little speckled sea bass about the same size, so we had food for a couple of days. We divided them up equally and there was no wastage—the head, body and bones were delicious. Everybody got an equal share.

The next day I had another sea gull land on my shoulder, which I caught, but didn't have the heart to wring his throat, and let him go. That night we ran into our first rain storm. Usually you try to avoid a black squall, but in this case we made it our business to get into it. We had no experience in catching water, but we used our shirts, socks and handkerchiefs. We would get them soaked up and wring—I was the official wringer in our boat—wring them into the bailing bucket, a little rubber bucket, and I would mouth it out of that and force it into the compartments in the Mae West life vests and then we would ration it from there on.

For the first few days we were rationed on the basis of two sips per man. That is about one-half a jigger, and then we were able to catch more water and built up a supply.

During the storm Captain Cherry's boat went upside down and we lost all of our flares, medical first-aid kit, and other things and didn't get them back. The little boat broke away. They paddled after it and brought it back and tied it up again and we got through the storm.

On the night of the 11th this boy that died was getting very low and in spite of the fact that the temperature was 78 to 80 degrees and the water was warm, the waves were breaking over us continually, and because of the combination of wind it was like being doused with ice water. So I moved him over from the little boat into our boat and cuddled him like a mother would a child, trying to give him the benefit of the warmth of my body and did for two nights, particularly from midnight until daybreak. The mist was deadly. The night he died, in the evening, he wanted to get back into the little boat and we switched.

At about 3 a.m. I heard his final gasp. In spite of the fact that I had taken men out of burning race cars and airplanes, I have never had that experience before and I was afraid to make any decision until daylight. At 6 a.m. we pulled together. I examined him thoroughly and pronounced him dead. I asked two of the boys to double-check me, witness and verify my decision. We stripped him, lifted him overboard

These rubber rafts kept Rick and his companions afloat for over three weeks.

Five of the rescued men enjoy their first real meal in 22 days.
Captain Rickenbacker is third from left.

gently and he disappeared. It was rather a diffi-cult thing to do, one of the hardest jobs I have ever had to do.

Minds Began to Crack

That left the seven of us. One of the boys cut loose — the little engineer, Bartek, who was alone in the boat — the boys had switched and changed off on this night unbeknown to us — and the next morning he was probably three-fourths of a mile away. He decided by this time he wanted to get back. The cause of it I don't know, other than a mental upset. We tied up again and then the minds began to crack. I say to you that I know things about those men's lives that probably no other living soul knows. Any sins of commission or omission were confessed. The only thing that saved me was that I didn't get time to get started on my own life or I would probably be talking yet.

On the night of the seventeenth day or eve-ning we saw our first signs of life. Then we saw a pontoon single-engine plane about five miles away. We had been trying to keep on the alert and keep some one on the watch all the time with ears and eyes open day and night, which became more difficult as time went on. But this little plane went by probably five miles away. We waved frantically, yelled, which meant nothing. He went on by and didn't come back; it was rather heart-breaking.

The next day two of them came out and again they missed us. The following day there were four of them and they passed us up, two on either side, about four, five or six miles away, and though we were all tied together and the rafts were yellow, it is probably one of the most difficult things in the world to see that small an object when the breakers are in action. As I said before, we didn't know where we were; we knew no one else knew. Most of the boys were afraid that we might die and no one would ever know whether we were dead or alive, as is still the case with Amelia Earhart, because that is a terrifically big ocean.

I thought we had landed west of our original destination. The only thing we had to go by was a watch, one watch — the others all went haywire on account of the salt water. We checked the rise and setting of the sun. To try to keep our drift, we worked up a sail with a shirt and the oars, and our drift was in a southwesterly direction, but we didn't know how much so. I was afraid we were heading for a group of Japanese-held islands and we had a double fear of being captured and made prisoners. We knew we wouldn't last long under these circumstances.

The night of the twentieth day, under protest, we broke up. Everybody went their own way. Captain Cherry in the little boat alone, with the co-pilot, navigator and the radio operator in the other boat. In my opinion, we couldn't have — the three men couldn't have lasted another forty-eight hours.

Captain Cherry was found by the machinist's mate in this one plane, the Navy plane, and the other three boys drifted on to an unoccupied island and were on it for one and one-half days

when the natives from another island found
them.

Boat Sighted by Two Planes

In the afternoon our boat was sighted. We saw
the two boys go by and then they came back
from the sun direction and they hit us right on
the nose. One of them came down and circled
very low and waved. I could see the smile on his
face. I waved back frantically to let him know
we were not dead, and then they went off over
the horizon. I found out later they were about
out of gas, but they came back about an hour
later. In the meantime a squall blew up and they
lost us. About thirty minutes later they came
back through it and hit us right on the nose.
One of them stayed there and circled and circled
while the other one left. The sun kept going
down and the fear was that, if he didn't land
soon, he would not be able to and we would be
lost again. About that time it was two-thirds
dark, the sun had gone then. I couldn't see how

he could possibly land without cracking up. He let go with a flare, his Very pistol, then a minute later another one; then over the horizon we saw the blinkers of a boat, which turned out to be a PT boat, and then he came down and landed — one of those unbelievable landings — and taxied up to us.

The ensign showed the strength of a Hercules in getting Colonel Adamson up the ten-foot lift in a bouncing plane and into the cabin, and the little engineer and myself on the wing. They lashed us to the body with our feet hanging over the leading edge. We started to taxi for the base some forty miles away. I don't remember how long we had gone, some fifteen or twenty minutes, when the PT boat, which had dashed madly from some fifty miles away, came up. It was decided to take two of us off and put us on the PT boat and then the plane followed another PT boat, which came up in the meantime, into the base because it was difficult to move Colonel Adamson and he was a very sick man, in addition. They got into the base and found out that

Captain Cherry had been picked up and we heard that the other three boys had landed on this unoccupied island, that the Navy was sending a doctor over to the island and that they would be brought in the following day.

Fortunately for us, the small Navy medical unit had just finished a little eight- or ten-cot hospital under the beautiful palm trees. The moonlight and palms made a picture that really reminded me of the stories you read about the South Sea isles. It was a Shangri-La, if there ever was one. They worked day and night on us. When I got in the PT boat I had gotten four big mugs of water and a big mug of beef broth before the doctor caught up with me. When we got to the base we were put on a couple of ounces every other hour. I tried to convince them that I could take it and it wouldn't harm me, but orders are orders and we had to obey, which probably was the right thing, because within forty-eight hours they sent some PBY boats. They picked us up and took us to the medical base, the Navy hospital in the Samoans

—all but the engineer and the radio operator, who were very weak and couldn't be moved.

Stayed with MacArthur

That is when Colonel Adamson ran into his serious illness. Fortunately for me, I bounced back, and in just two weeks, through the cooperation of our good Secretary and General Arnold, there was a new ship and crew sent out from the States that arrived on Sunday, and I left to complete my mission. On Monday I followed through and got into New Guinea and found the boys there doing a most unbelievable job, because everything they do and have done in the way of transportation was done by air—troop movements, gun movements, ammunition, supplies, evacuating the wounded, and under the most adverse conditions.

I stayed with General MacArthur and found one of the greatest enthusiasts for aviation that I had ever met, Lieutenant General George Kenney, who was in command of the air and one of the hardest hitting airmen we have anywhere in the world. The boys are working day and night; they have very difficult conditions under which to work.

The day I left they brought down nineteen enemy planes in one combat and three in another and lost only one. It was a mixture of heavy, medium and bombardment planes, of bombers and Zero fighters.

Whereas our quality and experience level is going up, there the Japanese airmen's experience level is going downhill very rapidly. There are left very few first-team pilots which are hard to beat, and they are tough. They go in anywhere at any time into combat, but it is quite evident, and our boys recognize it, that the great majority of Japanese pilots are inexperienced and green.

Four P-38s were showing up extremely well in combat, and particularly in bombardment of the units that Japs have at Buna and Gona. While out there I ran into the fact that Brigadier General Hanford ("Jack") MacNider, while lead-

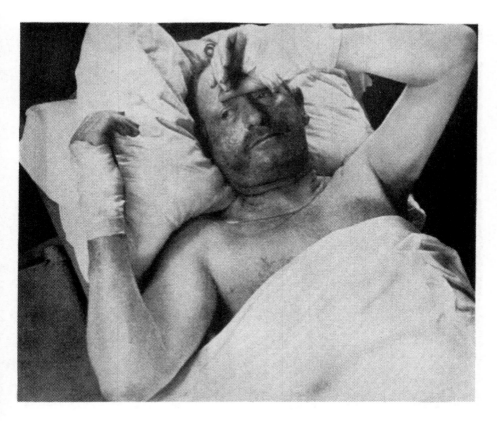

*His hands bandaged and on a stretcher, Colonel Hans C. Adamson
is moved to a South Pacific base hospital following his rescue.*

*Home again, Captain Rickenbacker is greeted by General Arnold
as Mrs. Rickenbacker looks on.*

ing one of his patrols during the night, had been hit by splinters from a hand grenade and was evacuated back to a hospital at Brisbane. I went to see him and found him the typical Jack that he always has been, not seriously wounded and on his way to recovery. He had a splinter in one eye, but they were able to relieve him of that.

He said that he had never found any ground troops any harder combat troops than the Japanese were. They just had no regard for their lives, and they would not be taken prisoners. If you want them you had to kill them, and I say to you very frankly our boys are learning very rapidly how to do that job, and they are doing it well.

Made Trip to Guadalcanal

I knew of certain things that were going to happen, that have since shown up in results. I came back and went up to Guadalcanal. They wouldn't let me in with my ship: I had to go up with a combat crew in a B-17 and there found a real hell-hole of mud and corruption. If only our people back home could know what those boys are doing for us and for future generations, I think we would take this war much more seriously.

The airmen are doing the same job, and both the Navy boys and the Army boys are blasting enemy ships, shooting Zeros out of the air at a rate of about four for one, and the B-17's are bringing down somewhere between nine and ten for one. They are destroying a tremendous amount of shipping and Japanese man-o-war cruisers and destroyers.

The difficulties in and under which our boys are operating in the air make it serious from a health angle, certain things that cannot be overcome. It has to be done, it is war. They are fighting malaria very seriously and constantly, and in my opinion if it weren't for the fact that they are having that stimulus—successes in combat—they could not possibly last physically nor mentally very long. But due to the great stimulus of winning, the success they have had, they are all happy and anxious to keep going.

One thing we need above everything else is

more and more; after seeing those boys in the air and on the ground, working as they are, twenty-four hours the clock around in the most unbelievable living conditions, I have come to the conclusion that if you brought a combat troop back to America, if you could overnight, and transfer them and put them into the factories and transfer the present war workers out into their positions, you would have your production doubled in thirty days' time. I mean that!

If only we could get the American people to realize that by even a small amount of additional effort to bring, to increase production of planes and equipment, ships, to get them supplies, ammunition, guns, gasoline, we will have served a great purpose.

The cries and objections to being rationed on rubber and gasoline seem so insignificant and ridiculous when we see what those boys haven't got. I couldn't help but think of the fact that the old rubber in an old rubber tire was sufficient to make up two or three of the type of rafts that we were in, and if people only knew that the saving of one old rubber tire makes it possible to produce one of those rafts which might be responsible, as it has been in our case, of saving seven men, they might take it more seriously. They might not worry so much about whether they had their automobiles on week-ends or whether they had to walk or ride the street-car or subway. Those of us on the home front must remember that we are 3,000 to 6,000 miles away from all of these hell-holes of fire. It is difficult for a man to imagine what our boys are doing without seeing, but with all the security and comforts of home we are enjoying, I hope that each will resolve to do even better.

I hope that the trip, what hardships we had to accept or endure may prove to be a lesson to the people back home in the stimulus to drive them on to greater peak, because without their effort and the material they are producing, our boys can't do the job they are so willing and anxious to do in the four corners of the world.

BIOGRAPHY

EDWARD VERNON RICKENBACKER, famed World War I ace, adventurer, author, and business executive, was born in Columbus, Ohio, in 1890. He was well known as an automobile racer when he accompanied General Pershing to France in 1917. Transferred to the Air Service, he became commander of the crack 94th Aero Pursuit Squadron, first U. S. Air Unit to take part on the Western Front. The Squadron was credited with 69 victories—largest of any American air outfit. Eddie Rickenbacker himself was credited with 26 of these victories.

Retired with the rank of Major, the Distinguished Service Cross (nine palms), Congressional Medal of Honor and many other decorations, he settled back into private life, becoming associated with Eastern Airlines as president and general manager. But when World War II came, Eddie Rickenbacker was ready for service again.

Captain Rickenbacker was sent on a special mission, was reported missing in October, and hope was practically gone when the Navy sent out the welcome flash that his pilot had been found. Next day the world knew that "indestructible" Eddie Rickenbacker and six of the men with him had been rescued.

CPSIA information can be obtained
at www.ICGtesting.com
Printed in the USA
BVHW091218160222
629175BV00005B/79

KESSINGER PUBLISHING

WWW.KESSINGER.NET

Thoughts

ON PEOPLE, PLANET, & PROFIT

AMY DOMINI